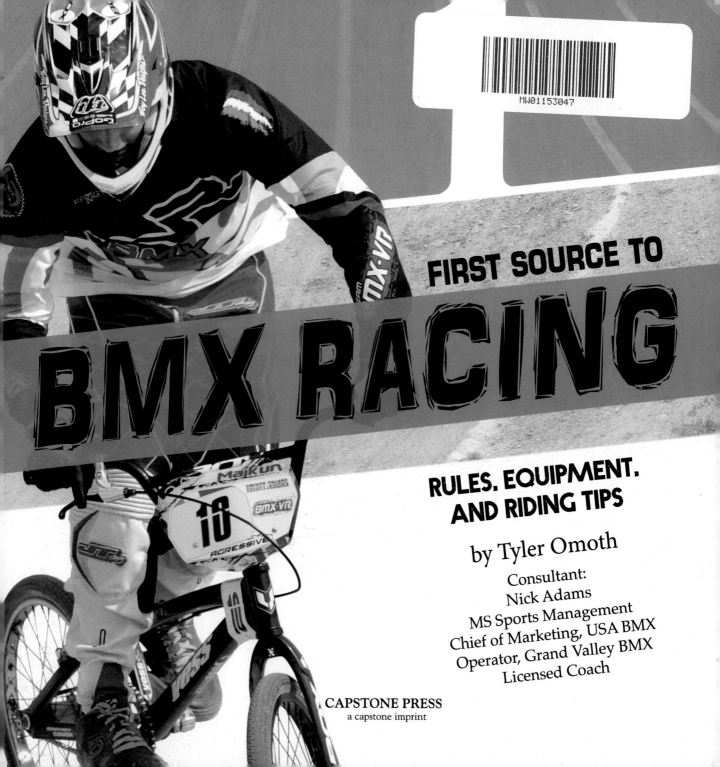

# FIRST SOURCE TO

# BMX RACING

## RULES, EQUIPMENT, AND RIDING TIPS

by Tyler Omoth

Consultant:
Nick Adams
MS Sports Management
Chief of Marketing, USA BMX
Operator, Grand Valley BMX
Licensed Coach

CAPSTONE PRESS
a capstone imprint

First Facts are published by Capstone Press,
1710 Roe Crest Drive, North Mankato, Minnesota 56003
www.mycapstone.com

Copyright © 2018 by Capstone Press, a Capstone imprint. All rights reserved. No part of this
publication may be reproduced in whole or in part, or stored in a retrieval system, or transmitted
in any form or by any means, electronic, mechanical, photocopying, recording, or otherwise,
without written permission of the publisher.

**Library of Congress Cataloging-in-Publication Data**
Names: Omoth, Tyler, author.
Title: First Source to BMX Racing : Rules, Equipment, and Key Riding Tips/
By Tyler Omoth.
Description: North Mankato, Minnesota : An imprint of Capstone Press, 2018. |
    Series: First Facts. First Sports Source | Includes bibliographical references and index. |
    audience: Age 7-9. | Audience: K to Grade 3.
Identifiers: LCCN 2016059567| ISBN 9781515787822 (library binding : alk. paper) |
    ISBN 9781515787846 (pbk. : alk. paper) | ISBN 9781515787907 (ebook pdf : alk. paper)
Subjects: LCSH: Bicycle motocross—Juvenile literature.
Classification: LCC GV1049.3 .O66 2018 | DDC 796.6/22—dc23
LC record available at https://lccn.loc.gov/2016059567

**Editorial Credits**
Bradley Cole editor; Sarah Bennett and Katy LaVigne, designers; Eric Gohl, media researcher;
Kathy McColley, production specialist

**Photo Credits**
Alamy Stock Photo: Reuters, 15; Dreamstime: Chris Van Lennep, 13, Homydesign, 19, Steirus, 17;
Newscom: MCT/Jeff Siner, 11, UPI/Matthew Healey, 5; Shutterstock: Aigars Reinholds, cover
(background), 1 (background, top), homydesign, 1 (background, bottom), 20 (right), 21 (right),
MarcelClemens, cover, 1, 9, Modfos, 20 (left), Robertomas, 7, 21 (left)

Design Elements: Shutterstock

Printed and bound in the United States of America.
001480

# TABLE OF CONTENTS

# Get in the Race!

Imagine your feet on the pedals. You zip around corners. You land jumps like Olympic gold medalist Connor Fields. Bicycle Motocross, or BMX, racing is popular in the United States, Canada, Australia, and other countries. It's full of action, sharp turns, and lots of jumps. Grab your helmet and get ready to ride!

## FROM PRETEND TO PRO RACER

Scot Breithaupt is the founder of BMX. At age 13, he and his friends rode their bikes in an empty dirt lot. They pretended to race motorcycles. The game caught on and grew into BMX racing.

### FACT
BMX racing officially became an Olympic sport in 2008. There is a men's and women's division.

CONNOR FIELDS

"I know I might be biased, but I think BMX is so cool and one of the best sports in the world!"
–U.S. gold medalist Connor Fields

5

# Get Ready to Ride!

## Equipment

BMX bikes are like regular bikes with a few changes. They have small **frames**. BMX bikes usually have 20-inch (51-centimeter) wheels. Most have only one **gear** and one brake. Since BMX bikes are used for racing, they are made of light metals, such as aluminum. A lighter bike can go faster.

**FACT**
Most professional or Olympic BMX races last less than 1 minute. Beginning races may take longer.

**frame**—the main part of the bicycle to which other parts are attached

**gear**—a toothed wheel that is connected to another toothed wheel; gears can be changed to control the amount of roll out or force applied by pedaling

## Safety Equipment

BMX racing involves high speeds and jumps. It is important to have the right safety equipment. A regular bike helmet isn't enough. For BMX racing you need a full helmet that protects your head and face. Safety goggles protect your eyes from flying rocks and dirt. Gloves, kneepads, and elbow pads can protect you during **wipeouts**.

### FACT
BMX riders must have at least an approved helmet, long-sleeved shirt, and pants. Elbow pads and jerseys give added protection, but they are not required.

**wipeout**—a fall or crash

## The Track

BMX racetracks are
usually made of dirt.

**FACT**
A standard BMX track is 900 to
1,300 feet (300 to 400 meters)
long. It has a starting gate and
a finish line.

They have many jumps and turns. The **starting
gate** is at the top of a large ramp or hill. Riders
use this to build up speed for the race. Many
tracks have three sharp turns. They look like a
giant "M" or "W" from above.

## BEST IN THE WORLD

The Union Cycliste Internationale BMX World Championships
is a major BMX competition. Randy Stumpfhauser has earned
a total of 12 medals — more than any other racer.

**10**  starting gate—the place where a race is started; the gate has room
for eight riders and ensures that all riders get a fair start

11

# CHAPTER 2

# How the Race Works

## Competitors

A BMX race has three separate parts called motos. The best riders in each moto advance to the next one.

Each rider sits at his or her own starting gate to begin. Riders compete in two or three **qualification heats**. The top eight racers compete for first place.

**FACT**
There may be more or fewer qualification heats depending on how many riders are competing.

**12**    qualification heat—one of several early races that determine which riders advance to future qualifying rounds or the main event

## Obstacles

A BMX track is full of **obstacles**. Rollers are small bumps in the track. They may be grouped together to form a bumpy "rhythm" section that slows down riders. A step-up is a small hill followed by a larger hill. A step-down is a large hill followed by a smaller hill.

**obstacle**—something a BMX rider jumps or rides over

Riders try to get through obstacles quickly. The track is set up to help them. A table top jump has a flat top. Riders can land on top if they can't jump to the other side. In a rhythm section, jumps are spaced so riders can **maneuver** through it smoothly. Sharp **banks** let racers take corners without slowing down.

## FREESTYLE

BMX racing quickly led to BMX freestyle riding. In BMX freestyle riders soar off large jumps. They perform stunts in the air.

**maneuver**—to move in a planned and controlled way that requires practiced skills

**bank**—the angle of the track; if a track has a high bank, the top of the track is much higher than the bottom of the track

**FACT**
BMX bikes do not have kick stands.
Racers do not need them and they
only add extra weight to the bike.

# CHAPTER 3
# Basic Rules

It is against the rules to bump other riders on purpose to try to crash them or slow them. But BMX riders often bump into one another by accident.

Rules guide other parts of a race too. On the final stretch, a racer cannot block another racer who may have more speed built up. If a racer accidentally leaves the track, that racer must re-enter the track as soon as it is safely possible.

"You can reach your goal if you believe in your dreams."

*–BMX Olympic gold medalist Mariana Pajón*

**FACT**
Mariana Pajón began racing BMX bikes at 4 years old. She competed in the 2012 and 2016 Olympics in women's BMX racing for Colombia. She won the gold medal both times.

# CHAPTER 4

# Riding Tips

Now that you're ready to ride, you can give it a try. These riding tips can help you race for first place.

## STARTING GATE

Being fast out of the starting gate can give you a great advantage. Try starting with both feet on the pedals while balancing, so when the gate drops you'll be ready to go.

## JUMPS

It may be tempting to try to jump as high as you can, but low jumps keep up your speed.

## LANDING

When tracks have a series of jumps, try to land on the downward slope of a jump. You'll keep up your speed.

## WARM UP

Make sure you're warmed up and stretched before a race so you are ready to give it your all.

## FACT

Rear brakes are best for BMX races. Front brakes could cause the bike to flip.

# Glossary

**bank** (BAYNK)—the angle of the track; if a track has a high bank, the top of the track is much higher than the bottom of the track

**frame** (FRAYM)—the main part of the bicycle to which other parts are attached

**gear** (GEER)—a toothed wheel that is connected to another toothed wheel; gears can be changed to control the amount of roll out or force applied by pedaling

**maneuver** (muh-NOO-ver)—to move in a planned and controlled way that requires practiced skills

**obstacle** (OB-stuh-kuhl)—something a BMX rider jumps or rides over

**qualification heat** (kwahl-i-fi-KAY-shun HEET)—one of several early races that determine which riders advance to future qualifying rounds or the main event

**starting gate** (STAHRT-ing GAYT)—the place where a race is started; the gate accommodates eight riders and ensures that all riders get a fair start

**wipeout** (WIPE-out)—a fall or crash

# Read More

**Adamson, Thomas K.** *BMX Racing.* Extreme Sports. Minneapolis: Bellwether Media, 2016.

**Butterfield, Moira and Kath Jewitt.** *Kids' Cycling Handbook: Tips, Facts and Know-How About Road, Track, BMX and Mountain Biking.* London: Carlton Kids, 2016.

**Challen, Paul.** *Bicycle Racing.* Checkered Flag. New York: PowerKids Press, 2015.

# Internet Sites

FactHound offers a safe, fun way to find Internet sites related to this book. All of the sites on FactHound have been researched by our staff.

Here's all you do:

Visit www.facthound.com

Type in this code: 9781515787822

Check out projects, games and lots more at
**www.capstonekids.com**

# Index